50 One Pot Wonder Recipes for Home

By: Kelly Johnson

Table of Contents

- Spaghetti and Meatballs
- Chicken Alfredo
- Beef Tacos

Chicken and Rice Casserole

Ingredients:

- 2 cups cooked chicken, shredded
- 1 cup cooked rice
- 1 can (10.5 oz) cream of mushroom soup
- 1 cup milk
- 1 cup shredded cheddar cheese
- 1/2 cup frozen peas
- 1/2 cup chopped onion
- 1/2 tsp garlic powder
- Salt and pepper to taste
- 1/2 cup breadcrumbs

Instructions:

1. **Preheat Oven:** Preheat oven to 375°F (190°C).
2. **Mix Ingredients:** In a bowl, combine chicken, rice, cream of mushroom soup, milk, cheese, peas, onion, garlic powder, salt, and pepper.
3. **Transfer to Dish:** Pour mixture into a greased baking dish.
4. **Top and Bake:** Sprinkle breadcrumbs over the top. Bake for 25-30 minutes, or until bubbly and the top is golden brown.
5. **Serve:** Serve hot.

Beef Stroganoff

Ingredients:

- 1 lb beef sirloin, sliced into strips
- 1 onion, chopped
- 2 garlic cloves, minced
- 1 cup mushrooms, sliced
- 1 cup beef broth
- 1 cup sour cream
- 2 tbsp flour
- 2 tbsp olive oil
- Salt and pepper to taste
- 2 cups egg noodles, cooked

Instructions:

1. **Cook Beef:** Heat olive oil in a large skillet over medium-high heat. Add beef and cook until browned. Remove and set aside.
2. **Cook Vegetables:** In the same skillet, add onion, garlic, and mushrooms. Cook until softened.
3. **Prepare Sauce:** Stir in flour and cook for 1 minute. Add beef broth and bring to a simmer.
4. **Combine Ingredients:** Return beef to the skillet and stir in sour cream. Cook until the sauce is creamy and beef is heated through.
5. **Serve:** Serve over cooked egg noodles.

One-Pot Pasta with Tomato Sauce

Ingredients:

- 12 oz pasta (penne, fusilli, or your choice)
- 1 can (14.5 oz) diced tomatoes
- 1 cup tomato sauce
- 1 onion, chopped
- 2 garlic cloves, minced
- 1 cup vegetable or chicken broth
- 1 tbsp olive oil
- 1/2 tsp dried basil
- 1/2 tsp dried oregano
- Salt and pepper to taste
- 1/4 cup grated Parmesan cheese

Instructions:

1. **Cook Vegetables:** In a large pot, heat olive oil over medium heat. Add onion and garlic, and cook until softened.
2. **Add Pasta and Sauce:** Add pasta, diced tomatoes, tomato sauce, broth, basil, oregano, salt, and pepper to the pot. Bring to a boil, then reduce heat and simmer, stirring occasionally, until pasta is cooked and most of the liquid is absorbed.
3. **Serve:** Stir in Parmesan cheese and serve hot.

Creamy Chicken and Mushroom Risotto

Ingredients:

- 1 cup Arborio rice
- 2 cups chicken broth
- 1 cup cooked chicken, diced
- 1 cup mushrooms, sliced
- 1/2 cup white wine (optional)
- 1/2 cup grated Parmesan cheese
- 1/2 cup heavy cream
- 1/2 onion, chopped
- 2 garlic cloves, minced
- 2 tbsp olive oil
- Salt and pepper to taste

Instructions:

1. **Cook Vegetables:** In a large pan, heat olive oil over medium heat. Add onion and garlic, and cook until softened.
2. **Cook Mushrooms:** Add mushrooms and cook until browned.
3. **Prepare Risotto:** Stir in Arborio rice and cook for 1-2 minutes. Add white wine if using and cook until absorbed.
4. **Add Broth:** Gradually add chicken broth, stirring constantly, until rice is tender and creamy.
5. **Finish:** Stir in cooked chicken, Parmesan cheese, and heavy cream. Season with salt and pepper.
6. **Serve:** Serve hot.

One-Pot Chili

Ingredients:

- 1 lb ground beef
- 1 can (15 oz) kidney beans, drained and rinsed
- 1 can (15 oz) black beans, drained and rinsed
- 1 can (14.5 oz) diced tomatoes
- 1 cup beef broth
- 1 onion, chopped
- 2 garlic cloves, minced
- 1 tbsp chili powder
- 1/2 tsp cumin
- Salt and pepper to taste

Instructions:

1. **Cook Beef:** In a large pot, cook ground beef over medium heat until browned. Drain excess fat.
2. **Cook Vegetables:** Add onion and garlic to the pot and cook until softened.
3. **Add Ingredients:** Stir in beans, diced tomatoes, beef broth, chili powder, cumin, salt, and pepper.
4. **Simmer:** Bring to a boil, then reduce heat and simmer for 20-25 minutes.
5. **Serve:** Serve hot.

Garlic Butter Shrimp and Orzo

Ingredients:

- 1 lb shrimp, peeled and deveined
- 1 cup orzo pasta
- 4 tbsp butter
- 4 garlic cloves, minced
- 1/2 cup chicken broth
- 1/2 cup grated Parmesan cheese
- 2 tbsp olive oil
- Salt and pepper to taste
- Chopped parsley for garnish

Instructions:

1. **Cook Orzo:** Cook orzo according to package instructions. Drain and set aside.
2. **Cook Shrimp:** In a large skillet, heat olive oil over medium heat. Add garlic and cook until fragrant. Add shrimp and cook until pink and cooked through.
3. **Prepare Sauce:** Remove shrimp and set aside. In the same skillet, add butter and chicken broth, stirring until combined.
4. **Combine Ingredients:** Add cooked orzo to the skillet and toss to coat. Stir in Parmesan cheese and return shrimp to the skillet.
5. **Serve:** Garnish with chopped parsley and serve hot.

Moroccan Chicken Stew

Ingredients:

- 4 chicken thighs, bone-in and skinless
- 1 onion, chopped
- 2 garlic cloves, minced
- 1 cup carrots, sliced
- 1 cup chickpeas
- 1 can (14.5 oz) diced tomatoes
- 1 cup chicken broth
- 1/2 cup dried apricots, chopped
- 2 tbsp olive oil
- 1 tsp ground cumin
- 1 tsp ground cinnamon
- 1/2 tsp turmeric
- Salt and pepper to taste

Instructions:

1. **Brown Chicken:** Heat olive oil in a large pot over medium heat. Brown chicken thighs on both sides and remove.
2. **Cook Vegetables:** Add onion and garlic to the pot and cook until softened.
3. **Prepare Stew:** Stir in carrots, chickpeas, diced tomatoes, chicken broth, apricots, cumin, cinnamon, turmeric, salt, and pepper.
4. **Simmer:** Return chicken to the pot and simmer for 30-35 minutes, or until chicken is cooked through and tender.
5. **Serve:** Serve with couscous or rice.

Beef and Vegetable Stew

Ingredients:

- 1 lb beef stew meat, cubed
- 2 cups beef broth
- 2 cups potatoes, peeled and diced
- 1 cup carrots, sliced
- 1 cup celery, sliced
- 1 onion, chopped
- 2 garlic cloves, minced
- 1 cup frozen peas
- 2 tbsp olive oil
- 1 tbsp tomato paste
- 1 tsp dried thyme
- 1 tsp dried rosemary
- Salt and pepper to taste

Instructions:

1. **Brown Beef:** In a large pot, heat olive oil over medium-high heat. Brown beef on all sides and remove.
2. **Cook Vegetables:** Add onion and garlic to the pot and cook until softened. Stir in tomato paste and cook for 1 minute.
3. **Prepare Stew:** Add beef broth, potatoes, carrots, celery, thyme, rosemary, salt, and pepper. Return beef to the pot.
4. **Simmer:** Bring to a boil, then reduce heat and simmer for 45-60 minutes, or until beef and vegetables are tender.
5. **Add Peas:** Stir in frozen peas and cook for an additional 5 minutes.
6. **Serve:** Serve hot.

Creamy Tomato Basil Soup

Ingredients:

- 2 tbsp olive oil
- 1 onion, chopped
- 2 garlic cloves, minced
- 1 can (28 oz) crushed tomatoes
- 2 cups vegetable broth
- 1/2 cup heavy cream
- 1/4 cup fresh basil leaves, chopped
- 1/2 tsp sugar
- Salt and pepper to taste

Instructions:

1. **Cook Vegetables:** Heat olive oil in a large pot over medium heat. Add onion and garlic, cooking until softened.
2. **Add Tomatoes:** Stir in crushed tomatoes, vegetable broth, and sugar. Bring to a simmer and cook for 20 minutes.
3. **Blend Soup:** Use an immersion blender to puree the soup until smooth.
4. **Add Cream and Basil:** Stir in heavy cream and fresh basil. Season with salt and pepper.
5. **Serve:** Serve hot.

One-Pot Lemon Herb Chicken

Ingredients:

- 4 boneless, skinless chicken breasts
- 1 cup chicken broth
- 1/2 cup lemon juice
- 1 tbsp olive oil
- 1 tsp dried thyme
- 1 tsp dried rosemary
- 2 garlic cloves, minced
- Salt and pepper to taste

Instructions:

1. **Season Chicken:** Season chicken breasts with thyme, rosemary, salt, and pepper.
2. **Cook Chicken:** Heat olive oil in a large pot over medium heat. Add chicken breasts and cook until browned on both sides.
3. **Add Liquid:** Pour in chicken broth and lemon juice. Bring to a simmer.
4. **Simmer:** Cover and cook for 15-20 minutes, or until chicken is cooked through.
5. **Serve:** Serve with the cooking liquid spooned over the top.

Sausage and Peppers Pasta

Ingredients:

- 12 oz pasta (penne or rigatoni)
- 1 lb Italian sausage, sliced
- 1 bell pepper, sliced
- 1 onion, chopped
- 2 garlic cloves, minced
- 1 can (14.5 oz) diced tomatoes
- 1/2 cup chicken broth
- 1/2 tsp dried basil
- 1/2 tsp dried oregano
- 1/4 cup grated Parmesan cheese
- Salt and pepper to taste

Instructions:

1. **Cook Pasta:** Cook pasta according to package instructions. Drain and set aside.
2. **Cook Sausage:** In a large skillet, cook sausage over medium heat until browned. Remove and set aside.
3. **Cook Vegetables:** In the same skillet, add bell pepper, onion, and garlic. Cook until softened.
4. **Prepare Sauce:** Stir in diced tomatoes, chicken broth, basil, oregano, salt, and pepper. Bring to a simmer.
5. **Combine Ingredients:** Add cooked sausage and pasta to the skillet. Stir until well combined and heated through.
6. **Serve:** Sprinkle with Parmesan cheese and serve hot.

Chicken Tortilla Soup

Ingredients:

- 1 lb chicken breast, cooked and shredded
- 1 can (14.5 oz) diced tomatoes
- 1 can (15 oz) black beans, drained and rinsed
- 1 cup corn kernels
- 4 cups chicken broth
- 1 onion, chopped
- 2 garlic cloves, minced
- 1 tsp cumin
- 1/2 tsp chili powder
- 1/2 tsp paprika
- Salt and pepper to taste
- Tortilla strips for garnish
- Shredded cheese and chopped cilantro for garnish

Instructions:

1. **Cook Vegetables:** In a large pot, sauté onion and garlic over medium heat until softened.
2. **Add Ingredients:** Stir in diced tomatoes, black beans, corn, chicken broth, cumin, chili powder, paprika, salt, and pepper. Bring to a simmer.
3. **Add Chicken:** Stir in shredded chicken and cook until heated through.
4. **Serve:** Garnish with tortilla strips, shredded cheese, and chopped cilantro.

Mediterranean Chickpea Stew

Ingredients:

- 1 can (15 oz) chickpeas, drained and rinsed
- 1 can (14.5 oz) diced tomatoes
- 1 cup vegetable broth
- 1 bell pepper, chopped
- 1 onion, chopped
- 2 garlic cloves, minced
- 1 tsp ground cumin
- 1/2 tsp smoked paprika
- 1/2 tsp dried oregano
- 1/4 cup chopped fresh parsley
- Salt and pepper to taste

Instructions:

1. **Cook Vegetables:** In a large pot, sauté onion and garlic over medium heat until softened.
2. **Add Ingredients:** Stir in bell pepper, chickpeas, diced tomatoes, vegetable broth, cumin, paprika, oregano, salt, and pepper.
3. **Simmer:** Bring to a simmer and cook for 20 minutes.
4. **Finish:** Stir in fresh parsley and serve hot.

Beef and Bean Chili

Ingredients:

- 1 lb ground beef
- 1 can (15 oz) kidney beans, drained and rinsed
- 1 can (15 oz) black beans, drained and rinsed
- 1 can (14.5 oz) diced tomatoes
- 1 cup beef broth
- 1 onion, chopped
- 2 garlic cloves, minced
- 1 tbsp chili powder
- 1/2 tsp cumin
- Salt and pepper to taste

Instructions:

1. **Cook Beef:** In a large pot, cook ground beef over medium heat until browned. Drain excess fat.
2. **Cook Vegetables:** Add onion and garlic and cook until softened.
3. **Add Ingredients:** Stir in kidney beans, black beans, diced tomatoes, beef broth, chili powder, cumin, salt, and pepper.
4. **Simmer:** Bring to a boil, then reduce heat and simmer for 20-25 minutes.
5. **Serve:** Serve hot.

Spicy Sausage and Bean Soup

Ingredients:

- 1 lb spicy Italian sausage, sliced
- 1 can (15 oz) cannellini beans, drained and rinsed
- 1 can (14.5 oz) diced tomatoes
- 4 cups chicken broth
- 1 onion, chopped
- 2 garlic cloves, minced
- 1 tsp smoked paprika
- 1/2 tsp red pepper flakes (optional)
- Salt and pepper to taste

Instructions:

1. **Cook Sausage:** In a large pot, cook sausage over medium heat until browned. Remove and set aside.
2. **Cook Vegetables:** In the same pot, add onion and garlic. Cook until softened.
3. **Add Ingredients:** Stir in cannellini beans, diced tomatoes, chicken broth, paprika, red pepper flakes if using, salt, and pepper.
4. **Simmer:** Bring to a simmer and cook for 20 minutes.
5. **Finish:** Return sausage to the pot and heat through. Serve hot.

Shrimp and Sausage Jambalaya

Ingredients:

- 1 lb shrimp, peeled and deveined
- 1 lb Andouille sausage, sliced
- 1 cup long-grain rice
- 1 can (14.5 oz) diced tomatoes
- 1 cup chicken broth
- 1 onion, chopped
- 1 bell pepper, chopped
- 2 garlic cloves, minced
- 1 tsp paprika
- 1/2 tsp cayenne pepper (optional)
- 1/2 tsp dried thyme
- 1 bay leaf
- Salt and pepper to taste

Instructions:

1. **Cook Sausage:** In a large pot, cook sausage over medium heat until browned. Remove and set aside.
2. **Cook Vegetables:** In the same pot, add onion, bell pepper, and garlic. Cook until softened.
3. **Add Rice:** Stir in rice, paprika, cayenne pepper if using, thyme, bay leaf, salt, and pepper.
4. **Add Liquids:** Pour in diced tomatoes and chicken broth. Bring to a boil.
5. **Simmer:** Reduce heat, cover, and simmer for 20 minutes.
6. **Add Shrimp and Sausage:** Stir in shrimp and sausage. Cook until shrimp are pink and rice is tender.
7. **Serve:** Serve hot.

Chicken and Sausage Gumbo

Ingredients:

- 1 lb chicken thighs, cut into pieces
- 1 lb Andouille sausage, sliced
- 1/2 cup vegetable oil
- 1/2 cup all-purpose flour
- 1 onion, chopped
- 1 bell pepper, chopped
- 3 celery stalks, chopped
- 3 garlic cloves, minced
- 1 can (14.5 oz) diced tomatoes
- 4 cups chicken broth
- 1 tsp dried thyme
- 1/2 tsp paprika
- 1/2 tsp cayenne pepper (optional)
- 2 bay leaves
- 1 cup okra, sliced
- Salt and pepper to taste
- Cooked rice for serving

Instructions:

1. **Make Roux:** In a large pot, heat vegetable oil over medium heat. Stir in flour and cook, stirring constantly, until the mixture turns a deep brown color (about 15-20 minutes).
2. **Cook Vegetables:** Add onion, bell pepper, celery, and garlic to the roux. Cook until vegetables are tender.
3. **Add Meat:** Stir in chicken and sausage. Cook until chicken is browned.
4. **Add Liquids and Spices:** Stir in diced tomatoes, chicken broth, thyme, paprika, cayenne pepper, and bay leaves.
5. **Simmer:** Bring to a boil, then reduce heat and simmer for 45 minutes.
6. **Add Okra:** Add okra and cook for an additional 15 minutes.
7. **Serve:** Serve over cooked rice.

One-Pot Mac and Cheese

Ingredients:

- 2 cups elbow macaroni
- 2 cups shredded sharp cheddar cheese
- 1 cup shredded mozzarella cheese
- 2 cups milk
- 1/2 cup heavy cream
- 1/4 cup butter
- 2 tbsp all-purpose flour
- 1/2 tsp garlic powder
- 1/2 tsp onion powder
- Salt and pepper to taste

Instructions:

1. **Cook Pasta:** In a large pot, cook macaroni according to package instructions. Drain and set aside.
2. **Make Cheese Sauce:** In the same pot, melt butter over medium heat. Stir in flour and cook for 1-2 minutes.
3. **Add Dairy:** Gradually whisk in milk and cream. Cook until sauce begins to thicken.
4. **Add Cheese:** Stir in cheddar and mozzarella until melted and smooth.
5. **Combine Pasta:** Add cooked macaroni to the cheese sauce and stir to combine.
6. **Serve:** Serve hot.

Teriyaki Chicken and Rice

Ingredients:

- 1 lb chicken breasts, sliced
- 1/2 cup teriyaki sauce
- 1 tbsp olive oil
- 2 cups cooked rice
- 1 cup broccoli florets
- 1 cup snap peas
- 2 garlic cloves, minced
- 1 tbsp fresh ginger, minced
- 1/2 tsp sesame seeds (optional)

Instructions:

1. **Cook Chicken:** Heat olive oil in a large skillet over medium heat. Add chicken and cook until browned and cooked through.
2. **Add Vegetables:** Stir in broccoli, snap peas, garlic, and ginger. Cook until vegetables are tender.
3. **Add Sauce:** Stir in teriyaki sauce and cook for 2-3 minutes.
4. **Combine with Rice:** Serve over cooked rice and garnish with sesame seeds if desired.

Lentil and Vegetable Soup

Ingredients:

- 1 cup lentils, rinsed
- 1 onion, chopped
- 2 carrots, chopped
- 2 celery stalks, chopped
- 2 garlic cloves, minced
- 1 can (14.5 oz) diced tomatoes
- 4 cups vegetable broth
- 1 tsp dried thyme
- 1/2 tsp cumin
- 1/2 tsp paprika
- Salt and pepper to taste

Instructions:

1. **Cook Vegetables:** In a large pot, sauté onion, carrots, celery, and garlic over medium heat until softened.
2. **Add Ingredients:** Stir in lentils, diced tomatoes, vegetable broth, thyme, cumin, paprika, salt, and pepper.
3. **Simmer:** Bring to a boil, then reduce heat and simmer for 30-35 minutes, or until lentils are tender.
4. **Serve:** Serve hot.

One-Pot Chicken Alfredo

Ingredients:

- 2 cups fettuccine pasta
- 1 lb chicken breasts, sliced
- 2 tbsp olive oil
- 2 cups heavy cream
- 1 cup grated Parmesan cheese
- 2 garlic cloves, minced
- 1/2 tsp dried Italian seasoning
- Salt and pepper to taste

Instructions:

1. **Cook Chicken:** Heat olive oil in a large pot over medium heat. Add chicken and cook until browned and cooked through.
2. **Add Pasta and Cream:** Add pasta, heavy cream, garlic, Italian seasoning, salt, and pepper.
3. **Simmer:** Bring to a boil, then reduce heat and simmer, stirring occasionally, until pasta is cooked and sauce has thickened.
4. **Add Cheese:** Stir in Parmesan cheese until melted and well combined.
5. **Serve:** Serve hot.

Baked Ziti with Sausage

Ingredients:

- 12 oz ziti pasta
- 1 lb Italian sausage, sliced
- 1 jar (24 oz) marinara sauce
- 2 cups shredded mozzarella cheese
- 1/2 cup grated Parmesan cheese
- 1/2 cup ricotta cheese
- 1 egg
- 1 tsp dried basil
- Salt and pepper to taste

Instructions:

1. **Cook Pasta:** Cook ziti according to package instructions. Drain and set aside.
2. **Cook Sausage:** In a large skillet, cook sausage over medium heat until browned.
3. **Combine Ingredients:** In a large bowl, mix cooked ziti, sausage, marinara sauce, ricotta cheese, egg, basil, salt, and pepper.
4. **Bake:** Pour into a baking dish and top with mozzarella and Parmesan cheeses. Bake at 375°F (190°C) for 25-30 minutes, or until bubbly and golden.
5. **Serve:** Serve hot.

Chicken and Spinach Stuffed Shells

Ingredients:

- 12 jumbo pasta shells
- 1 cup cooked chicken, shredded
- 1 cup fresh spinach, chopped
- 1 cup ricotta cheese
- 1 cup shredded mozzarella cheese
- 1/2 cup grated Parmesan cheese
- 1 jar (24 oz) marinara sauce
- 1 egg
- 1 tsp dried basil
- Salt and pepper to taste

Instructions:

1. **Cook Shells:** Cook pasta shells according to package instructions. Drain and set aside.
2. **Prepare Filling:** In a large bowl, mix shredded chicken, spinach, ricotta cheese, 1/2 cup mozzarella cheese, Parmesan cheese, egg, basil, salt, and pepper.
3. **Stuff Shells:** Fill each shell with the chicken and spinach mixture.
4. **Bake:** Spread marinara sauce in the bottom of a baking dish. Arrange stuffed shells in the dish and top with remaining mozzarella cheese. Bake at 375°F (190°C) for 25-30 minutes.
5. **Serve:** Serve hot.

Italian Meatball Soup

Ingredients:

- 1 lb Italian meatballs (store-bought or homemade)
- 4 cups beef broth
- 1 can (14.5 oz) diced tomatoes
- 1 cup pasta (small shells or orzo)
- 1 cup spinach or kale
- 1 onion, chopped
- 2 garlic cloves, minced
- 1/2 tsp dried oregano
- 1/2 tsp dried basil
- Salt and pepper to taste

Instructions:

1. **Cook Meatballs:** In a large pot, heat meatballs in beef broth over medium heat.
2. **Add Vegetables:** Stir in diced tomatoes, pasta, spinach or kale, onion, garlic, oregano, basil, salt, and pepper.
3. **Simmer:** Bring to a boil, then reduce heat and simmer until pasta is cooked and meatballs are heated through.
4. **Serve:** Serve hot.

BBQ Chicken and Sweet Potatoes

Ingredients:

- 1 lb chicken breasts
- 2 large sweet potatoes, peeled and cubed
- 1 cup BBQ sauce
- 2 tbsp olive oil
- 1 tsp smoked paprika
- 1/2 tsp garlic powder
- Salt and pepper to taste
- Fresh parsley for garnish (optional)

Instructions:

1. **Preheat Oven:** Preheat your oven to 400°F (200°C).
2. **Prepare Chicken and Potatoes:** Toss sweet potatoes with olive oil, smoked paprika, garlic powder, salt, and pepper. Place in a baking dish.
3. **Add Chicken:** Brush chicken breasts with BBQ sauce and place them on top of the sweet potatoes.
4. **Bake:** Bake for 25-30 minutes, or until chicken is cooked through and sweet potatoes are tender.
5. **Serve:** Garnish with fresh parsley if desired and serve hot.

Creamy Lemon Garlic Chicken Pasta

Ingredients:

- 8 oz fettuccine pasta
- 1 lb chicken breasts, sliced
- 2 tbsp olive oil
- 3 cloves garlic, minced
- 1 cup heavy cream
- 1/2 cup grated Parmesan cheese
- Juice and zest of 1 lemon
- 1/2 tsp dried thyme
- Salt and pepper to taste
- Fresh parsley for garnish (optional)

Instructions:

1. **Cook Pasta:** Cook fettuccine according to package instructions. Drain and set aside.
2. **Cook Chicken:** In a large skillet, heat olive oil over medium heat. Add chicken and cook until browned and cooked through. Remove chicken from skillet and set aside.
3. **Make Sauce:** In the same skillet, add garlic and cook for 1 minute. Stir in heavy cream, Parmesan cheese, lemon juice, zest, thyme, salt, and pepper.
4. **Combine Pasta and Chicken:** Add cooked pasta and chicken to the skillet and toss to coat.
5. **Serve:** Garnish with fresh parsley if desired and serve hot.

Vegetable and Bean Stew

Ingredients:

- 1 cup mixed beans (canned or dried, pre-cooked)
- 1 onion, chopped
- 2 carrots, chopped
- 2 celery stalks, chopped
- 1 bell pepper, chopped
- 3 cloves garlic, minced
- 1 can (14.5 oz) diced tomatoes
- 4 cups vegetable broth
- 1 tsp dried thyme
- 1/2 tsp cumin
- 1/2 tsp paprika
- Salt and pepper to taste

Instructions:

1. **Cook Vegetables:** In a large pot, sauté onion, carrots, celery, bell pepper, and garlic over medium heat until softened.
2. **Add Beans and Liquids:** Stir in beans, diced tomatoes, vegetable broth, thyme, cumin, paprika, salt, and pepper.
3. **Simmer:** Bring to a boil, then reduce heat and simmer for 30 minutes.
4. **Serve:** Serve hot.

Pork and Apple Stew

Ingredients:

- 1 lb pork shoulder, cubed
- 2 apples, peeled, cored, and sliced
- 1 onion, chopped
- 2 carrots, chopped
- 2 celery stalks, chopped
- 2 cloves garlic, minced
- 1 cup chicken broth
- 1/2 cup apple cider
- 1 tsp dried sage
- 1/2 tsp cinnamon
- Salt and pepper to taste

Instructions:

1. **Cook Pork:** In a large pot or Dutch oven, brown pork cubes over medium heat. Remove and set aside.
2. **Sauté Vegetables:** In the same pot, add onion, carrots, celery, and garlic. Cook until softened.
3. **Combine Ingredients:** Return pork to the pot. Stir in apples, chicken broth, apple cider, sage, cinnamon, salt, and pepper.
4. **Simmer:** Bring to a boil, then reduce heat and simmer for 1 hour, or until pork is tender.
5. **Serve:** Serve hot.

One-Pot Chicken and Dumplings

Ingredients:

- 1 lb chicken breasts, diced
- 1 onion, chopped
- 2 carrots, chopped
- 2 celery stalks, chopped
- 3 cloves garlic, minced
- 4 cups chicken broth
- 1 cup frozen peas
- 1/2 cup heavy cream
- 1 cup all-purpose flour
- 1/2 cup milk
- 1 tbsp baking powder
- 1/4 cup butter
- 1 tsp dried thyme
- Salt and pepper to taste

Instructions:

1. **Cook Chicken and Vegetables:** In a large pot, sauté onion, carrots, celery, and garlic until softened. Add chicken and cook until browned.
2. **Add Broth and Simmer:** Stir in chicken broth, peas, and thyme. Bring to a boil, then reduce heat and simmer for 20 minutes.
3. **Make Dumplings:** In a bowl, mix flour, milk, baking powder, and butter to form a dough. Drop spoonfuls of dough into the stew.
4. **Cook Dumplings:** Cover and cook for an additional 15-20 minutes, or until dumplings are cooked through.
5. **Serve:** Serve hot.

Beef and Barley Soup

Ingredients:

- 1 lb beef stew meat, cubed
- 1 cup barley
- 1 onion, chopped
- 2 carrots, chopped
- 2 celery stalks, chopped
- 3 cloves garlic, minced
- 1 can (14.5 oz) diced tomatoes
- 4 cups beef broth
- 1 tsp dried thyme
- 1/2 tsp paprika
- Salt and pepper to taste

Instructions:

1. **Cook Beef:** In a large pot, brown beef over medium heat. Remove and set aside.
2. **Sauté Vegetables:** In the same pot, add onion, carrots, celery, and garlic. Cook until softened.
3. **Add Ingredients:** Return beef to the pot. Stir in barley, diced tomatoes, beef broth, thyme, paprika, salt, and pepper.
4. **Simmer:** Bring to a boil, then reduce heat and simmer for 45 minutes, or until beef and barley are tender.
5. **Serve:** Serve hot.

Thai Peanut Chicken and Noodles

Ingredients:

- 8 oz rice noodles
- 1 lb chicken breasts, sliced
- 2 tbsp vegetable oil
- 1 red bell pepper, sliced
- 1 cup shredded carrots
- 2 green onions, chopped
- 1/4 cup chopped cilantro
- 1/2 cup creamy peanut butter
- 1/4 cup soy sauce
- 2 tbsp rice vinegar
- 1 tbsp honey
- 1 tbsp sriracha (optional)
- 1 garlic clove, minced
- 1 tsp grated ginger

Instructions:

1. **Cook Noodles:** Cook rice noodles according to package instructions. Drain and set aside.
2. **Cook Chicken:** In a large skillet, heat vegetable oil over medium heat. Add chicken and cook until browned and cooked through. Remove chicken and set aside.
3. **Sauté Vegetables:** In the same skillet, add bell pepper and carrots. Cook until tender.
4. **Prepare Sauce:** In a bowl, whisk together peanut butter, soy sauce, rice vinegar, honey, sriracha, garlic, and ginger.
5. **Combine:** Return chicken to the skillet, add cooked noodles and sauce, and toss to coat.
6. **Serve:** Garnish with green onions and cilantro, and serve hot.

Creamy Broccoli Cheddar Soup

Ingredients:

- 4 cups broccoli florets
- 1 onion, chopped
- 2 cloves garlic, minced
- 3 cups chicken broth
- 1 cup heavy cream
- 2 cups shredded cheddar cheese
- 2 tbsp butter
- 2 tbsp all-purpose flour
- Salt and pepper to taste

Instructions:

1. **Cook Vegetables:** In a large pot, melt butter over medium heat. Add onion and garlic, and cook until softened.
2. **Add Broccoli:** Stir in broccoli and cook for 2 minutes.
3. **Add Broth and Simmer:** Pour in chicken broth and bring to a boil. Reduce heat and simmer until broccoli is tender (about 15 minutes).
4. **Blend Soup:** Use an immersion blender to puree the soup until smooth.
5. **Add Cream and Cheese:** Stir in heavy cream and cheddar cheese until melted and smooth. Season with salt and pepper.
6. **Serve:** Serve hot.

Chicken Enchilada Soup

Ingredients:

- 1 lb chicken breasts
- 1 onion, chopped
- 2 cloves garlic, minced
- 1 can (10 oz) enchilada sauce
- 1 can (14.5 oz) diced tomatoes
- 4 cups chicken broth
- 1 cup corn kernels
- 1 cup black beans, drained and rinsed
- 1 tsp ground cumin
- 1/2 tsp chili powder
- Salt and pepper to taste
- Shredded cheese and chopped cilantro for garnish

Instructions:

1. **Cook Chicken:** In a large pot, cook chicken breasts until fully cooked. Shred the chicken and set aside.
2. **Sauté Vegetables:** In the same pot, sauté onion and garlic until softened.
3. **Add Ingredients:** Stir in enchilada sauce, diced tomatoes, chicken broth, corn, black beans, cumin, chili powder, salt, and pepper.
4. **Simmer:** Bring to a boil, then reduce heat and simmer for 20 minutes.
5. **Combine:** Return shredded chicken to the pot and heat through.
6. **Serve:** Garnish with shredded cheese and chopped cilantro, and serve hot.

One-Pot Ratatouille

Ingredients:

- 1 eggplant, diced
- 1 zucchini, sliced
- 1 bell pepper, chopped
- 1 onion, chopped
- 3 cloves garlic, minced
- 1 can (14.5 oz) diced tomatoes
- 1/4 cup olive oil
- 1 tsp dried basil
- 1/2 tsp dried thyme
- Salt and pepper to taste

Instructions:

1. **Sauté Vegetables:** In a large pot, heat olive oil over medium heat. Add onion and garlic, and cook until softened.
2. **Add Vegetables:** Stir in eggplant, zucchini, bell pepper, and cook for 5 minutes.
3. **Add Tomatoes and Spices:** Add diced tomatoes, basil, thyme, salt, and pepper.
4. **Simmer:** Bring to a boil, then reduce heat and simmer for 30 minutes, or until vegetables are tender.
5. **Serve:** Serve hot.

Shrimp and Grits

Ingredients:

- 1 cup grits
- 2 cups chicken broth
- 1 cup milk
- 1 lb shrimp, peeled and deveined
- 4 slices bacon, chopped
- 2 cloves garlic, minced
- 1 tbsp lemon juice
- 2 tbsp butter
- 1/4 cup chopped green onions
- Salt and pepper to taste

Instructions:

1. **Cook Grits:** In a pot, bring chicken broth and milk to a boil. Stir in grits and reduce heat. Cook according to package instructions until thickened.
2. **Cook Bacon:** In a skillet, cook bacon until crispy. Remove bacon and set aside.
3. **Cook Shrimp:** In the same skillet, add garlic and cook for 1 minute. Add shrimp and cook until pink and cooked through. Stir in lemon juice and butter.
4. **Combine:** Stir cooked bacon into grits. Serve shrimp over the grits and garnish with green onions.
5. **Serve:** Serve hot.

Chicken Marsala

Ingredients:

- 1 lb chicken breasts, pounded thin
- 1/2 cup flour
- 2 tbsp olive oil
- 1 cup Marsala wine
- 1 cup chicken broth
- 1 cup sliced mushrooms
- 1/4 cup chopped parsley
- Salt and pepper to taste

Instructions:

1. **Dredge Chicken:** Dredge chicken breasts in flour, shaking off excess.
2. **Cook Chicken:** In a skillet, heat olive oil over medium heat. Add chicken and cook until browned on both sides. Remove and set aside.
3. **Cook Mushrooms:** In the same skillet, add mushrooms and cook until softened.
4. **Make Sauce:** Stir in Marsala wine and chicken broth. Bring to a boil, then reduce heat and simmer until sauce thickens.
5. **Combine:** Return chicken to the skillet and cook until heated through.
6. **Serve:** Garnish with chopped parsley and serve hot.

Beef and Cabbage Stir-Fry

Ingredients:

- 1 lb beef sirloin, thinly sliced
- 1/2 head of cabbage, shredded
- 2 carrots, julienned
- 2 cloves garlic, minced
- 1 tbsp soy sauce
- 1 tbsp hoisin sauce
- 1 tbsp vegetable oil
- 1/2 tsp sesame oil
- Salt and pepper to taste
- Sesame seeds for garnish (optional)

Instructions:

1. **Cook Beef:** In a large skillet or wok, heat vegetable oil over high heat. Add beef and cook until browned. Remove and set aside.
2. **Sauté Vegetables:** In the same skillet, add garlic, cabbage, and carrots. Cook until tender.
3. **Add Sauce and Beef:** Stir in soy sauce and hoisin sauce. Return beef to the skillet and toss to combine.
4. **Finish:** Drizzle with sesame oil and season with salt and pepper.
5. **Serve:** Garnish with sesame seeds if desired and serve hot.

Chicken and Rice Soup

Ingredients:

- 1 lb chicken breasts
- 1 cup cooked rice
- 1 onion, chopped
- 2 carrots, chopped
- 2 celery stalks, chopped
- 3 cloves garlic, minced
- 4 cups chicken broth
- 1 cup frozen peas
- 1 tsp dried thyme
- Salt and pepper to taste

Instructions:

1. **Cook Chicken:** In a large pot, cook chicken breasts until fully cooked. Shred the chicken and set aside.
2. **Sauté Vegetables:** In the same pot, add onion, carrots, celery, and garlic. Cook until softened.
3. **Add Broth and Simmer:** Stir in chicken broth, peas, and thyme. Bring to a boil, then reduce heat and simmer for 20 minutes.
4. **Combine:** Return shredded chicken and cooked rice to the pot. Heat through.
5. **Serve:** Season with salt and pepper and serve hot.

One-Pot Cajun Chicken Pasta

Ingredients:

- 8 oz penne pasta
- 1 lb chicken breasts, diced
- 2 tbsp Cajun seasoning
- 1 tbsp olive oil
- 1 red bell pepper, chopped
- 1 green bell pepper, chopped
- 1 onion, chopped
- 3 cloves garlic, minced
- 1 can (14.5 oz) diced tomatoes
- 1 cup heavy cream
- 1 cup chicken broth
- 1/2 cup grated Parmesan cheese
- Salt and pepper to taste
- Fresh parsley for garnish (optional)

Instructions:

1. **Cook Chicken:** In a large pot, heat olive oil over medium heat. Add chicken and Cajun seasoning, and cook until browned and cooked through. Remove and set aside.
2. **Sauté Vegetables:** In the same pot, add bell peppers, onion, and garlic. Cook until softened.
3. **Add Liquids:** Stir in diced tomatoes, heavy cream, and chicken broth.
4. **Cook Pasta:** Add penne pasta and bring to a boil. Reduce heat and simmer until pasta is cooked and the sauce has thickened.
5. **Combine:** Return chicken to the pot, stir in Parmesan cheese, and season with salt and pepper.
6. **Serve:** Garnish with fresh parsley if desired, and serve hot.

Stuffed Bell Pepper Soup

Ingredients:

- 1 lb ground beef
- 1 onion, chopped
- 2 cloves garlic, minced
- 1 red bell pepper, chopped
- 1 green bell pepper, chopped
- 1 can (14.5 oz) diced tomatoes
- 4 cups beef broth
- 1 cup cooked rice
- 1 tsp dried oregano
- 1/2 tsp dried basil
- Salt and pepper to taste
- Shredded cheese for garnish (optional)

Instructions:

1. **Cook Beef:** In a large pot, brown ground beef over medium heat. Drain excess fat.
2. **Sauté Vegetables:** Add onion, garlic, and bell peppers to the pot, and cook until softened.
3. **Add Ingredients:** Stir in diced tomatoes, beef broth, cooked rice, oregano, basil, salt, and pepper.
4. **Simmer:** Bring to a boil, then reduce heat and simmer for 20 minutes.
5. **Serve:** Garnish with shredded cheese if desired, and serve hot.

Sweet and Sour Pork

Ingredients:

- 1 lb pork tenderloin, cubed
- 1/2 cup all-purpose flour
- 2 tbsp vegetable oil
- 1 bell pepper, chopped
- 1 onion, chopped
- 1 cup pineapple chunks
- 1/2 cup rice vinegar
- 1/4 cup soy sauce
- 1/4 cup ketchup
- 1/4 cup brown sugar
- 1 tbsp cornstarch mixed with 2 tbsp water
- Salt and pepper to taste

Instructions:

1. **Dredge Pork:** Dredge pork cubes in flour, shaking off excess.
2. **Cook Pork:** In a large skillet, heat vegetable oil over medium heat. Add pork and cook until browned and cooked through. Remove and set aside.
3. **Sauté Vegetables:** In the same skillet, add bell pepper and onion. Cook until softened.
4. **Make Sauce:** In a bowl, mix rice vinegar, soy sauce, ketchup, and brown sugar. Stir into the skillet.
5. **Thicken Sauce:** Stir in cornstarch mixture and cook until sauce has thickened.
6. **Combine:** Return pork and pineapple chunks to the skillet and heat through.
7. **Serve:** Serve hot over rice.

Chicken and Corn Chowder

Ingredients:

- 1 lb chicken breasts, diced
- 4 cups chicken broth
- 1 cup milk
- 2 cups frozen corn
- 1 onion, chopped
- 2 cloves garlic, minced
- 2 potatoes, peeled and diced
- 1/4 cup flour
- 2 tbsp butter
- 1 tsp dried thyme
- Salt and pepper to taste

Instructions:

1. **Cook Chicken:** In a large pot, cook chicken until fully cooked. Remove and set aside.
2. **Sauté Vegetables:** In the same pot, melt butter and sauté onion and garlic until softened.
3. **Add Ingredients:** Stir in flour and cook for 1 minute. Add chicken broth, milk, potatoes, and corn.
4. **Simmer:** Bring to a boil, then reduce heat and simmer until potatoes are tender.
5. **Combine:** Return chicken to the pot and stir in thyme. Season with salt and pepper.
6. **Serve:** Serve hot.

Beef and Mushroom Stroganoff

Ingredients:

- 1 lb beef sirloin, sliced
- 1 cup mushrooms, sliced
- 1 onion, chopped
- 2 cloves garlic, minced
- 1 cup beef broth
- 1 cup sour cream
- 2 tbsp flour
- 2 tbsp butter
- 1 tbsp olive oil
- 1 tsp dried thyme
- Salt and pepper to taste
- Cooked egg noodles for serving

Instructions:

1. **Cook Beef:** In a large skillet, heat olive oil over medium-high heat. Add beef and cook until browned. Remove and set aside.
2. **Sauté Vegetables:** In the same skillet, add butter, onions, and garlic. Cook until softened. Add mushrooms and cook until browned.
3. **Make Sauce:** Stir in flour and cook for 1 minute. Gradually add beef broth, stirring constantly.
4. **Simmer:** Bring to a simmer and cook until sauce thickens.
5. **Combine:** Return beef to the skillet and stir in sour cream and thyme. Season with salt and pepper.
6. **Serve:** Serve over cooked egg noodles.

One-Pot Spaghetti Carbonara

Ingredients:

- 8 oz spaghetti
- 4 oz pancetta or bacon, diced
- 2 cloves garlic, minced
- 1 cup grated Parmesan cheese
- 2 large eggs
- 2 cups chicken broth
- Salt and pepper to taste
- Fresh parsley for garnish (optional)

Instructions:

1. **Cook Pancetta:** In a large pot, cook pancetta or bacon until crispy. Remove and set aside.
2. **Sauté Garlic:** In the same pot, add garlic and cook for 1 minute.
3. **Add Broth and Spaghetti:** Stir in chicken broth and bring to a boil. Add spaghetti and cook according to package instructions until al dente.
4. **Make Sauce:** In a bowl, whisk together eggs and Parmesan cheese.
5. **Combine:** Remove pot from heat and quickly stir in egg mixture until creamy. Return pancetta to the pot. Season with salt and pepper.
6. **Serve:** Garnish with fresh parsley if desired and serve hot.

Mediterranean Chicken and Rice

Ingredients:

- 1 lb chicken breasts, diced
- 1 cup rice
- 2 cups chicken broth
- 1 cup cherry tomatoes, halved
- 1/2 cup Kalamata olives, sliced
- 1/4 cup feta cheese, crumbled
- 1/4 cup chopped fresh basil
- 2 cloves garlic, minced
- 2 tbsp olive oil
- Salt and pepper to taste

Instructions:

1. **Cook Chicken:** In a large pot, heat olive oil over medium heat. Add chicken and cook until browned and cooked through. Remove and set aside.
2. **Sauté Garlic:** In the same pot, add garlic and cook for 1 minute.
3. **Add Rice and Broth:** Stir in rice and chicken broth. Bring to a boil, then reduce heat and simmer until rice is cooked.
4. **Combine:** Stir in cherry tomatoes, olives, and cooked chicken. Cook until tomatoes are softened.
5. **Finish:** Stir in feta cheese and basil. Season with salt and pepper.
6. **Serve:** Serve hot.

Beef Tacos with Cilantro Rice

Ingredients:

- 1 lb ground beef
- 1 onion, chopped
- 2 cloves garlic, minced
- 1 tbsp taco seasoning
- 1 cup cooked rice
- 1/4 cup chopped cilantro
- 8 small taco shells
- Shredded lettuce, diced tomatoes, and shredded cheese for toppings

Instructions:

1. **Cook Beef:** In a skillet, cook ground beef with onion and garlic until browned. Stir in taco seasoning.
2. **Prepare Rice:** In a bowl, mix cooked rice with chopped cilantro.
3. **Assemble Tacos:** Fill taco shells with beef mixture and top with shredded lettuce, diced tomatoes, and shredded cheese.
4. **Serve:** Serve tacos with cilantro rice on the side.

Chicken Pot Pie Soup

Ingredients:

- 1 lb chicken breasts, diced
- 2 tbsp olive oil
- 1 onion, chopped
- 2 cloves garlic, minced
- 3 carrots, sliced
- 2 celery stalks, chopped
- 1 cup frozen peas
- 4 cups chicken broth
- 1 cup heavy cream
- 1/4 cup all-purpose flour
- 1 tsp dried thyme
- 1 tsp dried rosemary
- Salt and pepper to taste
- 1 cup pie crust pieces (optional, for garnish)

Instructions:

1. **Cook Chicken:** In a large pot, heat olive oil over medium heat. Add chicken and cook until browned. Remove and set aside.
2. **Sauté Vegetables:** In the same pot, add onion, garlic, carrots, and celery. Cook until vegetables are softened.
3. **Make Soup Base:** Stir in flour and cook for 1 minute. Gradually add chicken broth and bring to a boil.
4. **Simmer:** Reduce heat and simmer for 15 minutes. Stir in peas and cook for 5 more minutes.
5. **Add Cream and Seasonings:** Stir in heavy cream, thyme, rosemary, salt, and pepper. Return chicken to the pot and heat through.
6. **Serve:** Garnish with pie crust pieces if desired and serve hot.

Creamy Cajun Shrimp Pasta

Ingredients:

- 8 oz fettuccine pasta
- 1 lb shrimp, peeled and deveined
- 2 tbsp Cajun seasoning
- 2 tbsp olive oil
- 1 onion, chopped
- 3 cloves garlic, minced
- 1 cup heavy cream
- 1/2 cup chicken broth
- 1/2 cup grated Parmesan cheese
- 1/4 cup chopped fresh parsley
- Salt and pepper to taste

Instructions:

1. **Cook Pasta:** Cook fettuccine according to package instructions. Drain and set aside.
2. **Cook Shrimp:** In a large skillet, heat olive oil over medium heat. Add shrimp and Cajun seasoning. Cook until shrimp are pink and cooked through. Remove and set aside.
3. **Sauté Vegetables:** In the same skillet, add onion and garlic. Cook until softened.
4. **Make Sauce:** Stir in heavy cream and chicken broth. Bring to a simmer and cook until slightly thickened.
5. **Combine:** Stir in Parmesan cheese and cooked pasta. Return shrimp to the skillet and heat through.
6. **Serve:** Garnish with parsley and serve hot.

Veggie and Quinoa Stew

Ingredients:

- 1 cup quinoa, rinsed
- 4 cups vegetable broth
- 1 onion, chopped
- 2 cloves garlic, minced
- 2 carrots, chopped
- 2 celery stalks, chopped
- 1 zucchini, diced
- 1 cup corn kernels
- 1 cup diced tomatoes
- 1 tsp dried oregano
- 1 tsp dried basil
- Salt and pepper to taste

Instructions:

1. **Cook Quinoa:** In a large pot, bring vegetable broth to a boil. Add quinoa, reduce heat, and simmer for 15 minutes.
2. **Sauté Vegetables:** In another pot, sauté onion, garlic, carrots, and celery until softened.
3. **Add Ingredients:** Stir in zucchini, corn, diced tomatoes, oregano, basil, salt, and pepper.
4. **Combine:** Add cooked quinoa to the vegetable mixture and cook for 10 minutes.
5. **Serve:** Serve hot.

One-Pot Spanish Rice and Chicken

Ingredients:

- 1 lb chicken thighs, diced
- 1 cup rice
- 1 onion, chopped
- 2 cloves garlic, minced
- 1 red bell pepper, chopped
- 1 can (14.5 oz) diced tomatoes
- 1 cup chicken broth
- 1 tsp paprika
- 1 tsp dried oregano
- 1/2 tsp ground cumin
- Salt and pepper to taste
- Fresh cilantro for garnish (optional)

Instructions:

1. **Cook Chicken:** In a large pot, heat olive oil over medium heat. Add chicken and cook until browned. Remove and set aside.
2. **Sauté Vegetables:** In the same pot, add onion, garlic, and bell pepper. Cook until softened.
3. **Add Rice and Liquids:** Stir in rice, diced tomatoes, chicken broth, paprika, oregano, cumin, salt, and pepper.
4. **Simmer:** Bring to a boil, then reduce heat and cover. Simmer until rice is cooked and liquid is absorbed, about 20 minutes.
5. **Combine:** Return chicken to the pot and stir well. Garnish with fresh cilantro if desired.
6. **Serve:** Serve hot.

www.ingramcontent.com/pod-product-compliance
Lightning Source LLC
LaVergne TN
LVHW081342060526
838201LV00055B/2809